Table of Contents

1. Intro: Why I Wrote This 2
2. Why create your first website using WordPress? 3
3. Choosing the right web host. 3
4. Get A Domain Name 6
5. Connecting Domain and Hosting Together 6

On the next page add HostGator Nameserver which you have obtained in step 1 (above): 8

6. The 15 Minute Website Builder 8
7. Tweaking Your WordPress Setup 11
8. Ok Let's start tweaking the site 13
9. Upload your pictures, documents and more to the Media folder..14
10. Creating Your Pages & Post Content Using The New Block Editor For WordPress 2020 (Gutenberg) 16
11. Creating a "Home" page 24
12. Create a custom menu 25
13. Adding a Contact Us Form 26
14. Themes - Instantly change the look of your site 29
15. The Plugin Functionality Formula. 32
16. Plugins that I think you should install. 36
17. Selling Products and Services 39
19. How To Take Payments On Your WordPress Website Sales page 42
20. WordPress Simple PayPal Shopping Cart Plugin 42

Sell anything from your WordPress website easily. 42

Plugin Description 42

Screenshots 43

    Simple Product Display 43

21. Okay now about Stripe Payment Processor 44
22. Stripe WordPress Plugin 46
23. Quick Tips.. 47
24. Affiliate Marketing - No Product Needed!................... 48
25. Membership Sites 51
26. The Audience Capture Method 53
27. Traffic Generation 54
28. Last minute tips:... 58
29. Conclusion... 59
30. What's Next?... 59
31. Your Goal 60

1. Intro: Why I Wrote This

Hi, my name is Keith Junor and I have been creating WordPress websites for about 6 years.

I started out creating sites for myself to sell affiliate products (products created by other people and sold for a commission by others).

By the time you finish this guide you will be able to build your own WordPress websites to promote your company, sell any product or service or build these sites for others and get paid for it.

This is what I am going to show you today.

- How to choose a domain and webhost
- Connect them together
- Installing WordPress to your domain and hosting
- Tweaking it
- Adding media and content

- Adding a contact form
- Changing themes and adding plugins
- Setting up a sales page to sell any product or service
- Affiliate marketing with your site
- Getting traffic from social media sites
- Lead and traffic generation ideas

Now, before we get into details on how to create your WordPress website, you should know first....

2. Why create your first website using WordPress?

With WordPress, you don't have to be a certified genius or a hard-core geek to set it up.

The pages on your website do not need to be hand-coded. You do not need to spend money on any programmer or website

developer. You can update your very own website without any extra help.

There are three things you need to create a WordPress website:
1. A domain name (the name of your website)
2. A hosting account (this is where your website lives on the internet)
3. 30 minutes.

You could stop there and have a very basic WordPress site (more suitable for a blog website but also makes a good basic website.
To go to the next level and have a great site to promote your product or service here is some of what you need to learn:

- How to Choose the Best Web Hosting
- How to Register a Domain Name
- How to Install WordPress
- How to Change Your Theme
- How to Write Your First Blog Post
- How to Customize WordPress with Plugins
- Resources to Learn WordPress

3. Choosing the right web host.

Ok. Now you are going to learn how to choose the right hosting company for your domain/website

Hosting is what allows you to connect your Dot Com website name (also known as an URL or domain) to the internet so searchers can find it.

There are hundreds of them out there.
In fact, it took me around 2 weeks before I found the right one. It is not a good idea to just go for a cheap webhost.

You want to know that your host company offers a good quality service and the tools you need to run your blog effectively.

Some of the things you want to consider are:
Support
Your website may go down or face some issues.
That's normal.

What's frustrating is if it happens in the middle of the night, and there's no one to help you out.

Top priority: pick a web host with a customer support available 24/7. No kidding.

It's also important; the person assisting you is accommodating, friendly and knowledgeable.

It only adds to your disappointment if he or she is cold and doesn't possess the necessary skills to assist you solving your problem.

If you are a newbie you might be a little bit nervous about using WordPress.
But your web host actually holds the secret.
They can provide you with a one-click installation through an app called Fantastico.

Fantastico is an easy to use add-on provided by the webhosts, which allows one-click installation of many open source applications including WordPress.

You can also have full control over your website through its cPanel or Control Panel.

One of the common questions people ask me is this: what type of web host should I get?

Better yet, what type of plan?
Here's my suggestion, newbies. Go to
http://www.hostgator.com.

They have one of the most comprehensive plans I've seen.

I definitely love their baby plan, which guarantees unlimited domain, disk space, and bandwidth.

There's certainly room for growth for your blog site.
It also has an SSL certificate, which means all types of payment transactions are secured.

That's a big plus for Internet marketers since buyers would definitely like to protect their confidential information such as their name and credit card number.

If this isn't enough, you can get the plan for less than $10 a month.

4. Get A Domain Name

Next you are going to learn how to get a domain name.

Of course, you can never have a website without a domain. Consider it as your own address in cyberspace.

Like your personal home address, you want it to be easily remembered and spelled out for friends and guests.

You also want to keep it very short.
There are many places where you can buy your domain, which you can own for a year.

One I would recommend is GoDaddy.com and the other is called Namecheap.com. http://www.namecheap.com.

A domain will cost you around $12 a year, but if you're resourceful enough, such as looking for coupons in Google, you can reduce the price to almost $3.

Now that you have a domain name From Godaddy.com and website hosting from HostGator it's time to link them together.

5. Connecting Domain and Hosting Together

Ok, let's move on to connecting the domain and hosting together so your site can be found online when someone types in the name or clicks on a link to it.

Before you login to your GoDaddy dashboard, you need to find your HostGator hosting Name-server.

The Name-server detail will be in your Hostgator Welcome email, or you can login to the Hostgator cPanel (control panel) to find the Name-server.

Inside the cPanel, at the bottom you will find your Server I.P & name-server.

In this case, we only need Nameserver details. In this case the Name-servers are
- NS6377.hostgator.com • NS6378.hostagtor.com

Once you have your Hosting Name-server with you, all you need to do is: Login to your GoDaddy domain manager & change the domain name-server to point it to HostGator.

Here I have added the screenshot that shows the steps.

Login to your GoDaddy Dashboard:

On the domain manager page, select the domain name for which you need to change the domain name.

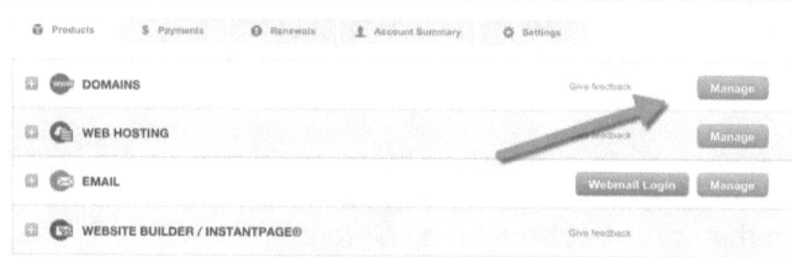

Click on Set Name-server which will bring up a screen like this:

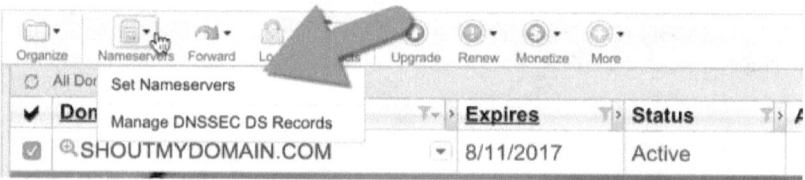

• Standard= Default GoDaddy Nameserver • Custom: Manually enter any nameserver

You need to select custom & click on Add nameserver:

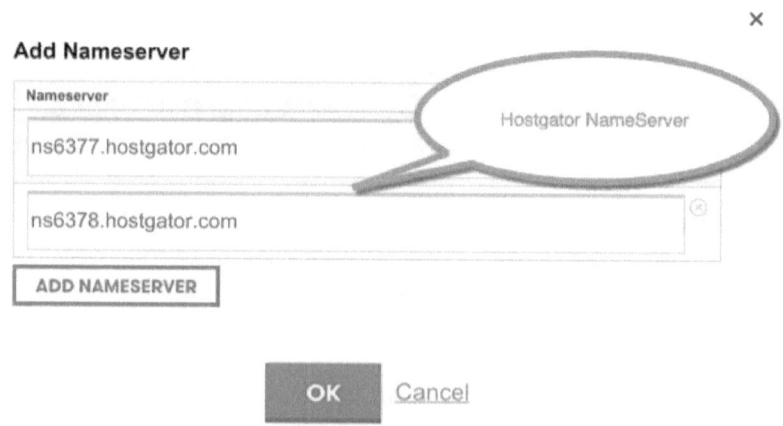

On the next page add HostGator Nameserver which you have obtained in step 1 (above):

Click on Ok & your GoDaddy domain will be pointed to your HostGator Hosting.

Note: When you update the domain Nameserver, it will take few minutes to hours for the Nameserver to propagate on the internet.

6. The 15 Minute Website Builder

Now we are at the most important but also one of the easiest steps of installing or setting up WordPress on your domain and hosting.

There are two ways to install WordPress: manually and a one click process through "Fantastico De Luxe".

Manual Installation is a very long process and a little complicated leaving room for error.

That is why I suggest you choose to use Fantastico.
Here's what you're going to do:
Step 1: You should have already signed up for a web hosting account (Hostgator.com).

Step 2: Once you have a web hosting account, you'll be provided with the username and password. You can use the information to log in to your cPanel.

At this point, open your cPanel.
The URL of your cPanel will be www.yourdomain.com/cpanel

Step 3: Look for the "Fantastico De Luxe" icon. Make sure that the web hosting account offers you this feature. Some don't, and you need to purchase it.

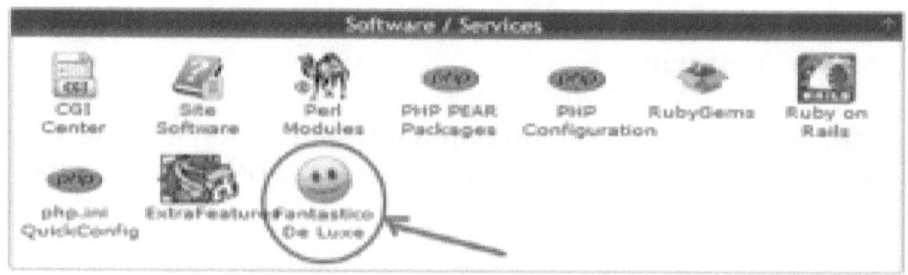

That's going to be costly at your end. The icon, by the way, is the one with a smiley face.

Step 4: Scroll down until you get to the Blogs section. Among the list, choose WordPress by ticking the box.

Step 5: At the right-hand side, you will see information about the type of WordPress version you're going to install.

It's important that you get the latest version.
Press "New Installation".

Step 6: You will then be redirected to the one-click installation process. This includes determining the Installation Location, Admin Access Database Configuration, and E-mail Account Configuration.

The Admin Access Data is the area where you're going to create the username and password for your WordPress site.

Base Configuration contains the details related to your website, such as your nickname or username.

You can be very creative about it, but it's best if you stick to your own personal name.

You will also create the name and description of your website (this can always be changed in the Dashboard of your new WordPress website).

Step 7: Press Finish Installation. You will then receive a notification confirming the successful setup of your WordPress website.

You have now completed the installation of WordPress onto your domain.

Just go to the url (domain name) you chose during the setup to see what the basic configuration of your new website looks.

Remember this is a great starting point for your first WordPress site but you can now change or improve the look and functionality of your website.

You also want to add your own individuality by changing the colors, add your own content etc.

In the chapter on THEMES I will be showing you how to change the look in a few clicks using 1 of hundreds of FREE themes.

7. Tweaking Your WordPress Setup

Now we are going to start tweaking your site in order to change the look and function of the basic site and to help get it to be listed in the search engines like Google.

Is it enough that you installed WordPress?

The answer is no. You need to do some tweaking for a number of reasons. First, you want your website to rank in search engines in order to get some free traffic to your website.

Secondly you will want to change the look and functionality as well as adding your own graphics, top header etc., to personalize your new website.

You don't have to be a Superman when you're tweaking. Start with the basics.
In order to make the changes to your site you need access to the admin panel.

Note: The instructions from this guide are referring to the WP Admin dashboard.

You can get to this dashboard by adding /wp-admin to the end of your site's URL/domain name (e.g. keithjunor.com/wp-admin)

Enter the username and password you chose when setting up WordPress in Fantastico Deluxe.

This opens the Dashboard that looks something like this.

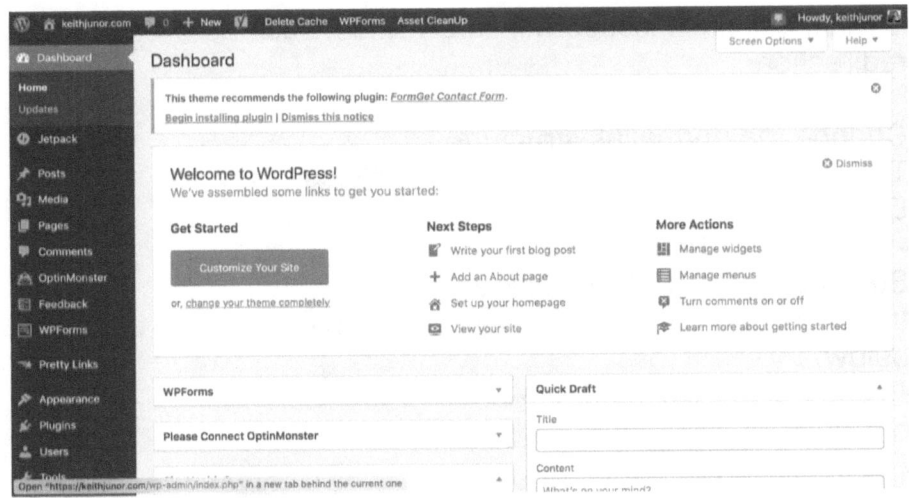

(yours will look different from the picture in that there are more items added to it)

8. Ok Let's start tweaking the site

Permalinks
Permalink means permanent link. This means it doesn't change. If the page gets listed in the search engines, like Google, it's the link that is listed.

Natural permalinks are composed of a series of characters—numbers and letters—that are unreadable. The default WordPress permalink looks like http://yourdomain.com/?p=ID.

That's why they are not considered user as well as search engine friendly.

The good news is you can change the permalink structure. The bad news is doing this after you have content on the site is not ideal since issues will surely arise, such as wrong redirection.

Change the permalink structure .
To set up your permalink, go to WordPress Admin -> Dashboard
-> Options -> Permalinks.
Select Customize Permalink Structure.
In my opinion the best permalinks options are any of the ones below:
/%category%/%postname%/
or
/%postname%/
or
/%postname%.htm

9. Upload your pictures, documents and more to the Media folder

Let me show you how to add a variety of media files such as graphics, video, word docs, audio tracks and more to your site.

You can either upload media files ahead of using them by uploading to your Media Library:

Here are instructions for you:

To add a new media item to your library, click the "Media" button.

From there, click add new then "select files" to upload a new image, video or any other media from your computer.

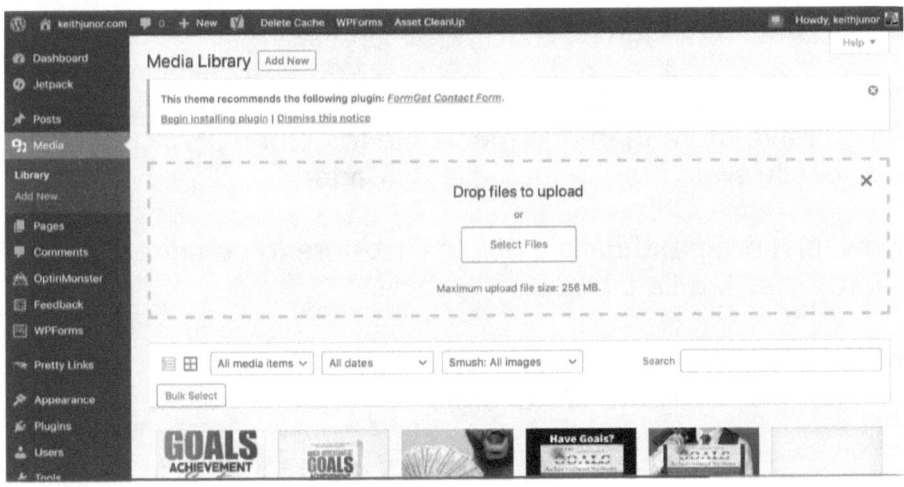

Once your image has been uploaded, you'll see it has been added to the library.

This is what the Media Library looks like:

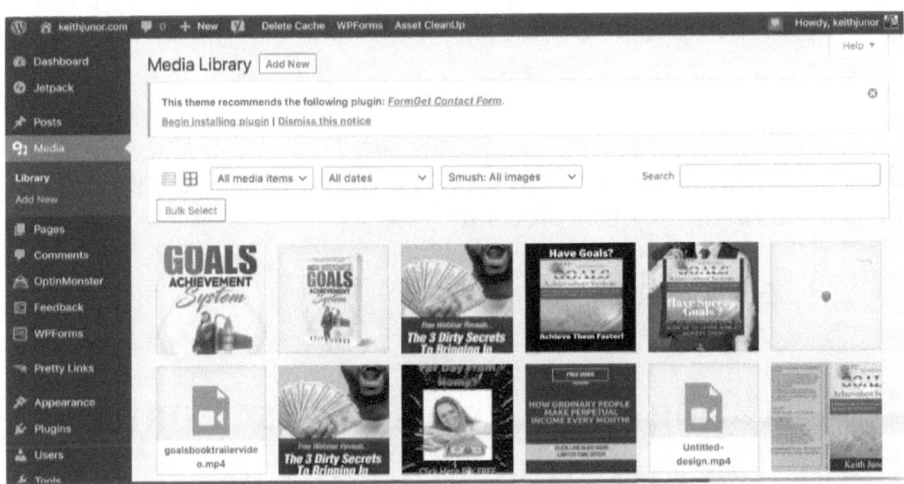

Editing Images in the WordPress Media Library

One of the neat features of the WordPress media library is the ability to edit images. Click on an image, then click the Edit Image button.

Now, you can crop, rotate, flip or scale the image.

WordPress Media Library Multi-File Uploader
If you have more than one media file to upload at once, you can easily switch to the multi-file uploader.

Now, just drag and drop multiple files here to be added to your WordPress Media Library.

NOTE: With the new Gutenberg Block Editor you can also add images while you are creating a post or page.

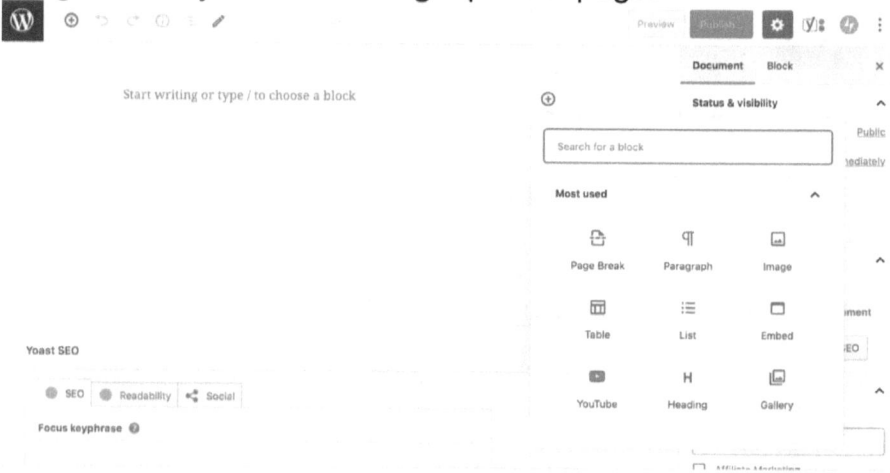

Just click the + button, then choose image and find the image in the Media library or upload it.

Lets talk more about:

10. Creating Your Pages & Post Content Using The New Block Editor For WordPress 2020 (Gutenberg)

How to Create your New Blog Post or Page

On the left side of your WordPress dashboard click on Posts - Add New menu. Then go to Pages - Add New.

This will launch the new block editor.

The top of every post or page starts with an area for the title

Then you can use the mouse to click below the title to start writing a new paragraph.

But if you want something besides a new paragraph just click on the add a new block button on the left top corner which will then show you some commonly used blocks as well as a search box, where you can type a keyword, and other choices to add.

Clicking on the button will show the add block menu with a search bar on top and commonly used blocks below.

The editor block comes with its own toolbar which appears on top of the block.

In the screenshot below we are working in a paragraph block showing basic formatting options: text alignment, bold, italic, insert-link, and strikethrough buttons.

You can just drag and drop blocks to move them or by clicking the up and down buttons.

Reusing Saved Blocks

Blocks you have entered content in can be saved and reused individually if you have content that you re-use in different pages or places on a page.

After you have written the content in that block, simply click on the menu ellipsis button (three dots vertically) located in the right corner of the block's toolbar.

In the menu choose the 'Add to reusable blocks' option.

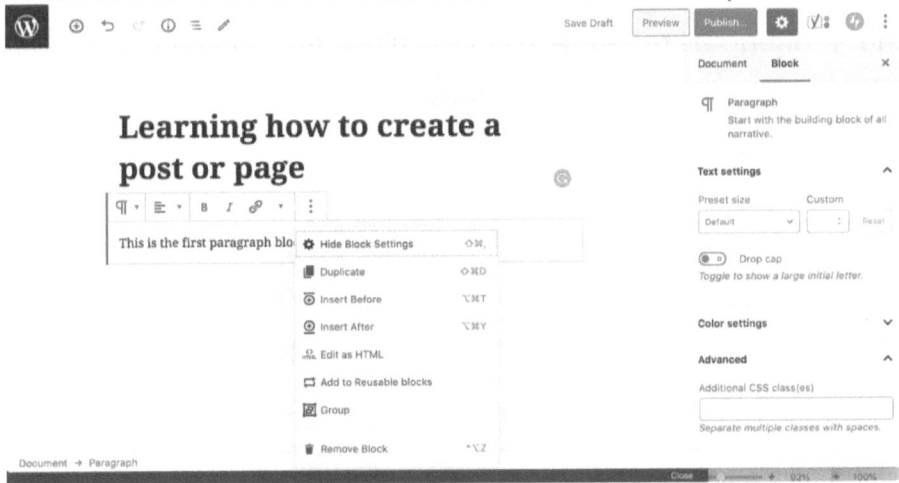

Enter a name for this block and then click on the save button.

You now have a reusable block.

Now that you have a reusable block I can show you how to add it to other WordPress posts and pages.

Choose the post or page that you want to use your reusable block on and then click on the add block button.

Find your saved block under the Reusable tab or by typing its name in the search bar and click on the name to add it into your page.

You are able to manage your reusable blocks by clicking on the -manage all reusable blocks- link where you can edit or delete any of your reusable blocks.

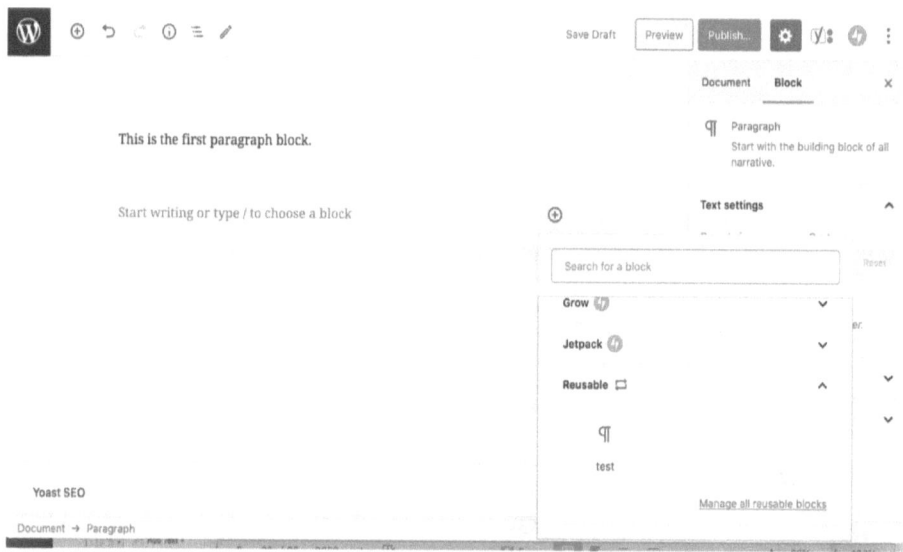

Each WordPress post contains a lot of metadata. This includes information like publish date, categories, tags and more.
All these options are neatly placed in the right column on the editor screen.

Plugin Options in The Block Editor

Some popular plugins are already integrated into the block editor.
For example, the best forms creator, WPForms, that allow you to add "Contact Us" form into your content is available in the widget content block.

Adding an image
Simply add the image block and then upload an image file from your computer, or drag and drop the media, or select from the media library.

After adding the image, you will be able to see the settings where you can add or change the size, add a clickable link to another page or website into the image.

Just click on the picture you added then click the little paperclip and add the link where it says "Paste URL or type to search" (if linking to a page or post in your website just type the name of the post or page title)

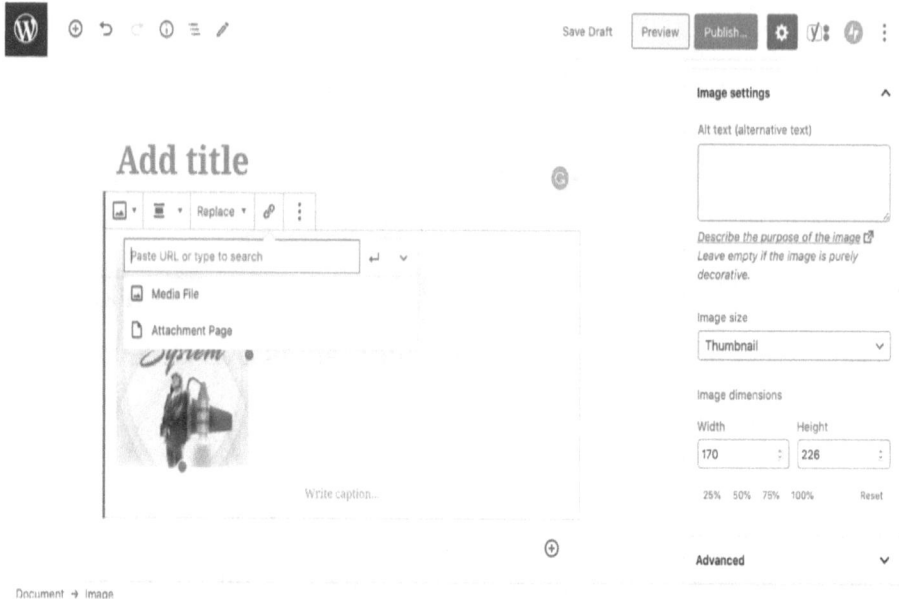

You can also change the size of the image or add alternative text to it as shown in the left side of the above image.

Adding a link to text or a paragraph

These blocks come with an insert link button in the toolbar, as well as lists the ability to create, numbered, bold type, strikethroughs and more.

Advanced Content Creation Techniques

Shortcodes
Basically, a shortcode is a small piece of code, indicated by brackets like [this], that performs a dedicated function on your site.

You can place it just about anywhere you'd like, and it will add a specific feature to your page, post, or other content.

With shortcodes, you can display forms, galleries, call-to-action buttons, or columns of content without the need for programming skills.

You can embed files (like google docs) or create objects

You get some shortcodes from plugins.

New Content Blocks in The Block Editor

1. Add an image next to some text in WordPress

You can do this with the media & text block.

This block opens with two blocks side-by-side allowing you to easily add an image and add some text next to it.

2. Adding a button

WordPress editor now comes with a button block so you can add a button in a variety of colors and 3 styles

You can create a link for your button, use a variety of colors, and you have a choice of three button styles.

3. Add cover images

A cover image is a wide image used as a cover for a new section of a page or for the beginning of a post.

You just add the cover block and upload the image you want.

You will mostly use an overlay color for the cover or make it a solid background color.

Creating tables in posts

In order to add tables, this editor comes with a default Table block, which makes it easy to add tables by simply adding the block and then selecting the number of columns and rows you want.

There two basic style options.

You can add data to table rows. You can add additional rows and columns as needed.

11. Creating a "Home" page

After you have created a few pages you need to decide which page or post you want visitors to land on when they type yourdomain.com.

The easiest way to do this is in settings- reading and then choose either "your latest posts" or "a static page" and then choose the page from the dropdown list.

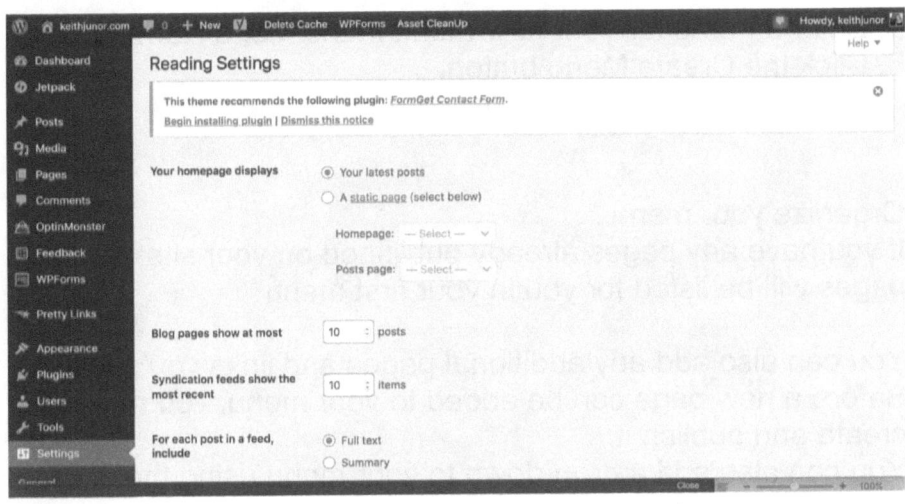

Be sure to click the" save changes down at the bottom of the page" button to save this setting.

12. Create a custom menu

This step involves creating a custom menu for the main pages of your site.

When you go to your website you may notice that you have two "home" links on your site menu, or that the pages on your site are not displayed in the order you wish.

The good news is that you can create a custom menu for your site in any arrangement you like.

1. Login to the WordPress Dashboard.
2. From the 'Appearance' menu on the left-hand side of the Dashboard, select the 'Menus' option to bring up the Menu Editor.
3. Select Create a new menu at the top of the page.

4. Enter a name for your new menu in the Menu Name box.
5. Click the Create Menu button.

Organize your menu
If you have any pages already published on your site, those pages will be listed for you in your first menu.

You can also add any additional pages and links you'd like. Before a new page can be added to your menu, you must first create and publish it.
You can also add a drop-down to your menu using the drag-and-drop feature.

1. Add the link to your menu that will appear in a drop-down list.
2. Drag it and drop it directly beneath the main menu item you want it to be found under.
3. Drag it again, this time to the right, so it indents beneath the main menu item, and drop it there.

Save your menu Once you have organized your menu, be sure to click the Save button to save your custom menu.

13. Adding a Contact Us Form

Now I am going to show you how to create a form page where people can enter their contact info and question and have it automatically emailed to you.

First go the wpforms tab on the right in the dashboard.

To create a new form to use just click "new form".
Choose 'simple contact form"

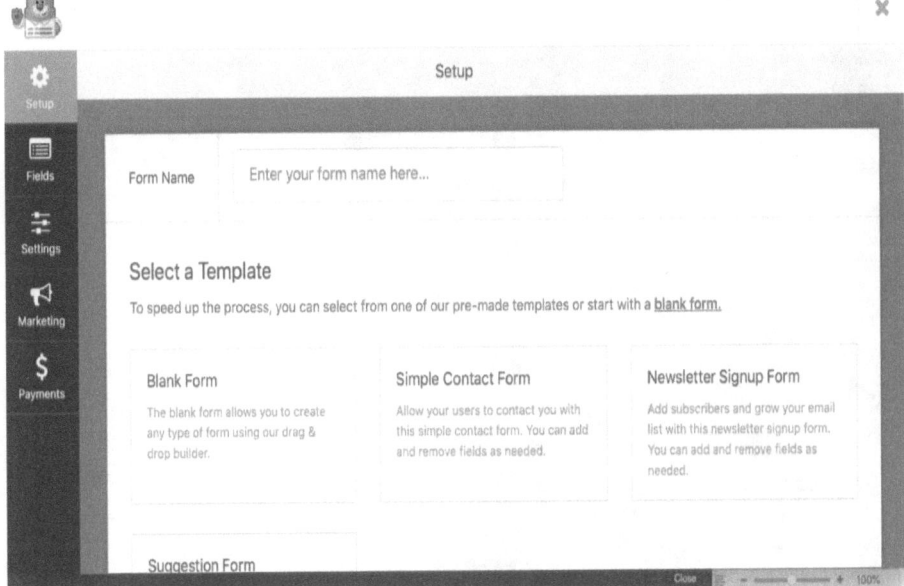

Then you can either accept the premade contact form or drag and drop different fields to create your own style for the info you want to collect.

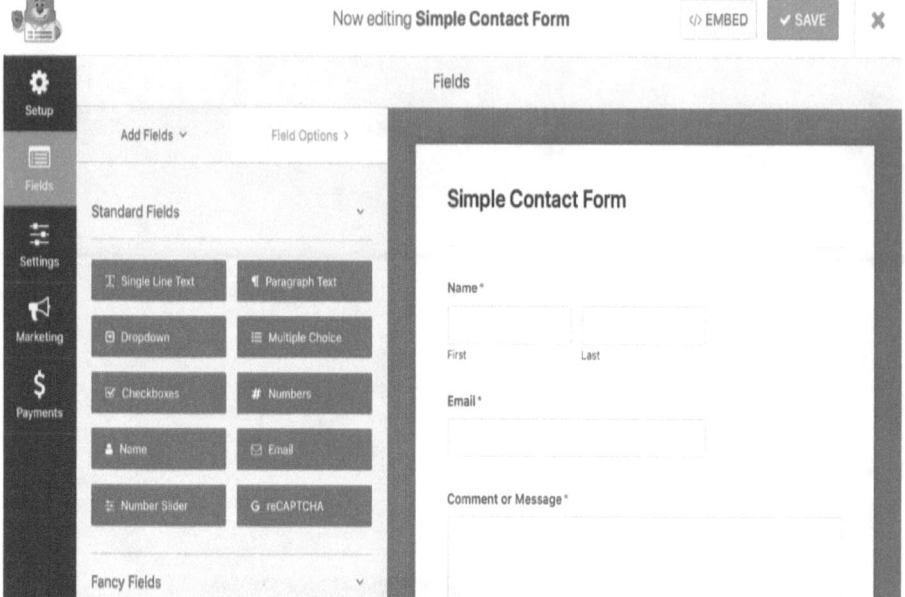

• Dropdown: creates a dropdown of options
• Email Address: requires an email address format • Name: text field
• Radio Button: similar to the checkbox field type

• Text: a single line of text • Text Area: several lines of text • Web Address: requires a URL format

Notification preferences When a user submits your contact form, it will be emailed to the owner/author of the website/post/page (to the email address that they have on file for their WordPress.com account and the subject line will be the title of your post.

Then you just create new page-Call it "contact us" and then choose a block and then choose "widgets" then "wpforms"

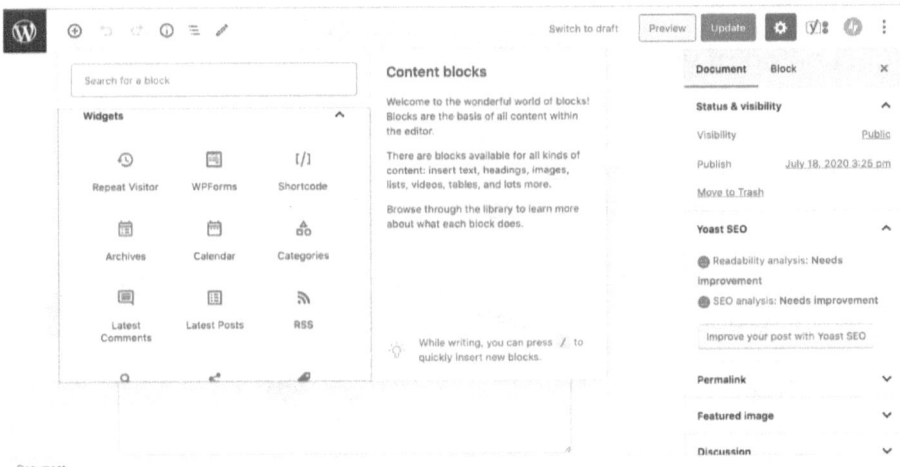

Then select your "contact us" form from the dropdown box labelled "Select a Form"

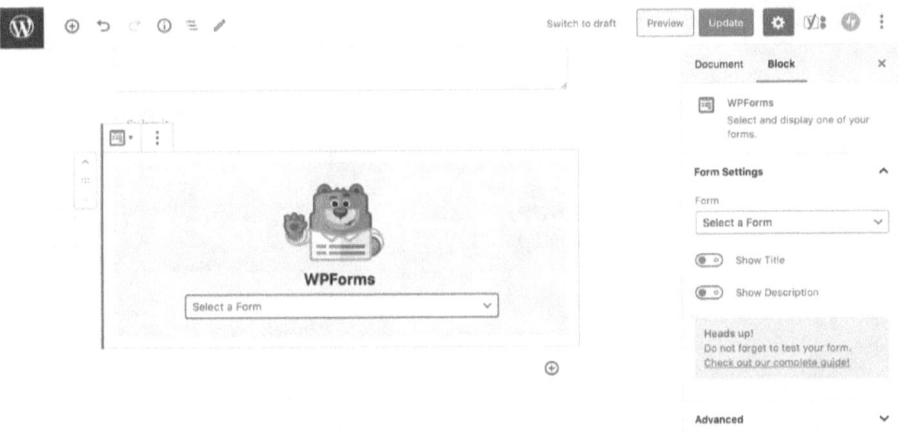

Now we come to one of the most important parts of creating your site.

14. Themes - Instantly change the look of your site

Now you are going to learn how to change the look of your site by changing the Theme.

Themes are a way of instantly changing the look, feel and functioning of your site.

Adding a theme
The theme adds aesthetic value to your website. WordPress already has plenty of themes to choose from.

To access them, open your account, go to your dashboard, click on Appearance, and select Themes

Once you find a theme you like click on it then choose either "Live Preview" (shows you what the theme looks like on your site), or "Activate" to make the changeover to the new theme.

Then you can always use the Customize button under Appearance to change things like color, layout etc.

Now if you find more free themes using Google then you will need to download them to your computer then upload and install to your site.

You can also find hundreds more free themes just using a Google search like "free WordPress themes".

I cannot include training on using advance themes as that would take a lot more pages, just get used to using the included themes first.

These more advanced themes will require a lot more knowledge to get them to look the way you want them too.

Just remember that after you have changed a theme you access it through the "Appearance tab on the left then choose customize to open the customizing window:

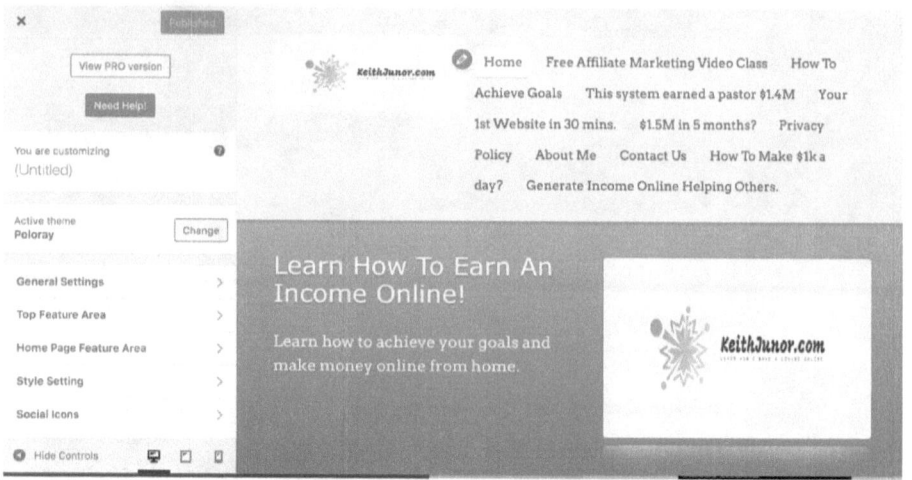

15. The Plugin Functionality Formula.

Let me now train you about Plugins that will extend and improve the functioning of your website.

I could never stress this enough.

WordPress has become so flexible because of the plugins and there are far too many to cover here.

Plugins are basically apps that allow WordPress to perform all kinds of functions.

Plugins are ways to extend and add to the functionality that already exists in WordPress.

The initial setup of a WordPress site starts off very lean so Plugins then offer custom functions and features so that each user can tailor their site to their specific needs.

To install a plugin:
Install a Plugin using WordPress Plugin Search

The easiest way of installing a WordPress plugin is to use the plugin search.

The only downside of this option is that a plugin must be in the WordPress plugin directory which is limited to only free plugins but you can add other plugins into the directory by uploading and installing them.

Adding a new plugin
First thing you need to do is go to your WordPress admin area and click on Plugins » Add New.

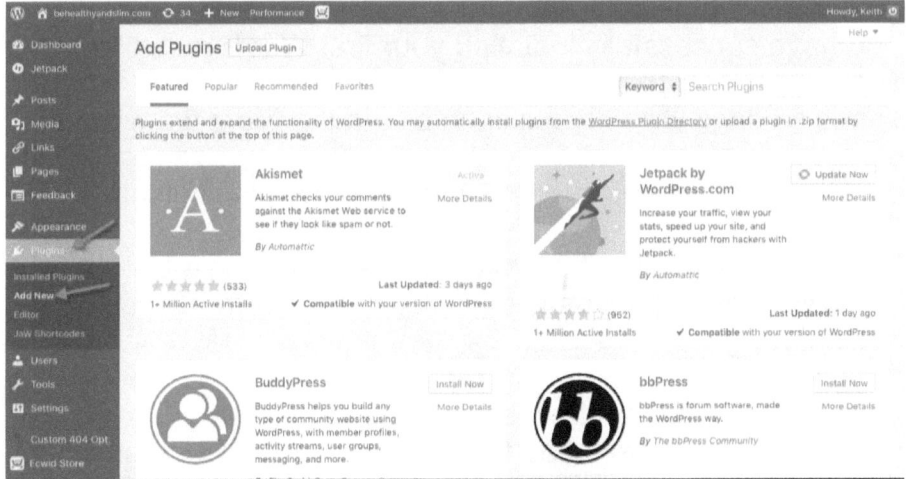

You will see a screen like the one in the screenshot above.

Find the plugin by typing the plugin name or the functionality you are looking like: Jetpack (one of my favorites because it contains
dozens of useful plugins such as TRACKING so you can see where your visitors are coming from every day).

If you do not have it installed click "Install Now".
Since I already have it installed it is requesting that I "Update" it.
When you click the 'Install Now' button WordPress will now download and install the plugin for you.

After this, you will see the success message with a link to activate the plugin or return to plugin installer.

A WordPress plugin can be installed on your site, but it will not work until you activate it.

So go ahead and click on the activate plugin link to activate the
plugin on your WordPress site.

That's all.

You have successfully installed your first WordPress plugin. The next step is to configure the plugin settings.
These settings will vary for each plugin therefore we will not be
covering that but this info is available in the plugin itself.

Install a Plugin using the WordPress Admin Plugin Upload
Paid WordPress plugins are not listed in the WordPress plugin directory.

These plugins cannot be installed using the first
method so WordPress has the Upload method to install such plugins.

We will show you how to install WordPress plugin using the upload option in the admin area.

First, you need to download the plugin from the source (which will be a .zip file).

Next, you need to go to WordPress admin area and visit Plugins
» Add New.
After that, click on the Upload Plugin button on top of the page.

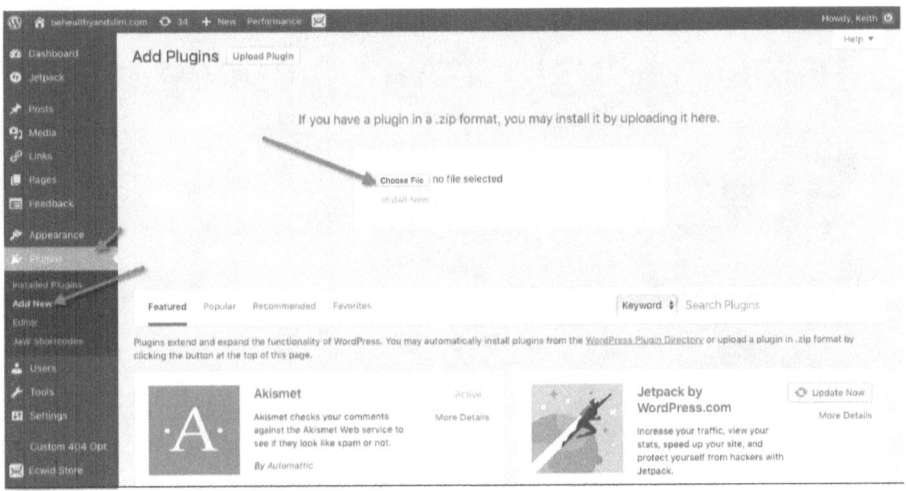

This will bring you to the plugin upload page. Here you need to click on the choose file button and select the plugin file you downloaded earlier to your computer.

After you have selected the file, you need to click on the install now button.

WordPress will now upload the plugin file from your computer and install it for you.

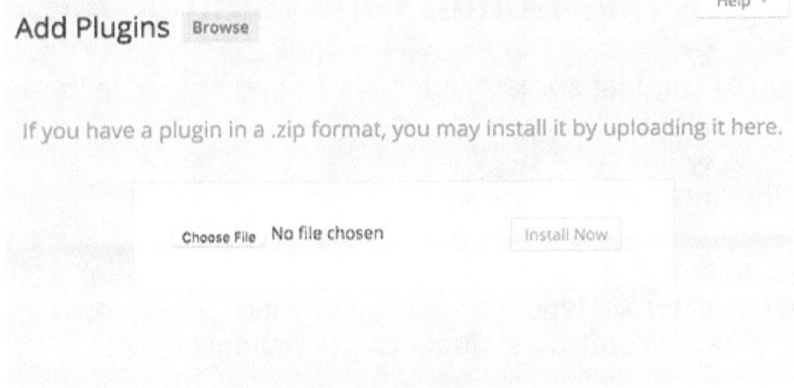

You will see a success message after installation is finished.

Installing Plugin from uploaded file:

Unpacking the package...

Installing the plugin...

Plugin installed successfully.

Activate Plugin | Return to Plugins page

Once installed, you need to click on the Activate Plugin link to start using the plugin.
You would have to configure the settings to fit your needs. These
settings will vary for each plugin therefore we will not be covering that in this post.

16. Plugins that I think you should install.

I am going to suggest some plugins I think you should install but they are not mandatory.

For me, they are some of the most essential ones.

I have found that if I need my website to have a particular functionality all I do is type into Google or Bing (now known as Microsoft Ads): "WordPress plugin to...(functionality you need)

Believe me that there are literally hundreds or thousands of plugins created by hundreds of developers so you have an excellent chance of finding the one you need.

Jetpack

(https://WordPress.org/plugins/jetpack/)- Jetpack simplifies managing WordPress sites by giving you visitor stats, security services, speeding up images, and helping you get more traffic.

Jetpack is a free plugin.

Traffic Growth & Insights
Jetpack tells you how many visits your site gets and helps you get more traffic with tools like Related Posts, Publicize, Enhanced Distribution, and Sharing.

Security
Jetpack protects your site against brute force attacks and unauthorized logins.

We also monitor your site for downtime and keep your plugins updated.

Image Performance
Jetpack automatically optimizes and speeds up images using the global WordPress.com content delivery network. This saves you hosting costs by reducing bandwidth.

Centralized Management
With Jetpack comes a centralized dashboard on WordPress.com. Manage plugins and menus, publish posts, and view enhanced site stats for all of your sites.

Jetpack includes other features that help you customize your site including Custom CSS, Contact Forms, Galleries and

Carousels, Notifications and Subscriptions, Configurable Widgets, and many more.

Search Engine Optimization

High Performance Seo Plugin (htttps://WordPress.org/plugins/gregs-high-performance-seo/) -This plugin is intended for anyone who wants to help search engines find website content.
Or this alternative:

All-in-one SEO Pack (http://WordPress.org/extend/plugins/all-in-one-seo-pack/) – Don't stress yourself when it comes to SEO. This is your ultimate superhero.

It improves and optimizes titles, meta tags and is designed to be compatible with WordPress e-commerce websites.

Akismet (http://WordPress.org/extend/plugins/akismet/) – This is a plug-in that traps spam comments. You don't want them in your website. Moreover, visitors hate spam, and they view any website with lots of it as completely unprofessional.

Google XML Sitemaps (http://WordPress.org/extend/plugins/google-sitemap-generator /) – What's a sitemap? It's simply a place where you can find all the pages on your website.

That's also the place search engine spiders crawl in, searching for pages to be listed so your website pages can be found on the web.

If you want your blog to be friendly to search engines and have as many pages indexed as possible, then you have to install Google XML Sitemaps.

You can control the URL, date of crawl, and other important information.

Google Analytics (http://WordPress.org/extend/plugins/google-analytics-for-wordpress) – This is one of the most important tools for Internet marketers. The bottom line of creating a weblog is to earn profits.

However, you will never get to that point if you don't understand your visitors in the first place.

Google Analytics helps you with that. It tells you how many visitors are going to your website, which pages are checked, what types of keywords are used to find your blog/pages/posts, how long they stayed etc.

They are useful because they help you in your marketing campaigns.

It will help you understand if you're driving the right types of people into your weblog, if the keywords are working well for you, or if you're getting the right click-through rate for your weblog.

WP Super Cache (http://WordPress.org/extend/plugins/wp-super-cache/) – You need this to load your pages faster.

In case you didn't know, Internet users stay for a very short time on any website.

If it doesn't load within 10 seconds, expect them to leave and never come back. Just follow the instructions that come with the plugin to speed up your site.

17. Selling Products and Services

Let's talk about selling products or services on your site.
Before you can actually start selling items, you need to have a very important thing:
A Sales Page.
The sales page doesn't sell the products per se.

For the customers to buy the items, they have to proceed to your website, go to the Shopping Cart, place an order, and pay through whatever means is shown on the shopping cart.

But your sales page is fundamental since it's your come-on page, the one that tells your leads why it's a good idea to buy items from you.

This is where majority of Internet marketers and sellers fail. They just don't know how to do it.

You may be a good writer when it comes to writing your own sales letter in a notepad or word document, but if you don't know how to make html page, those efforts will be completely futile.

The good news is WordPress makes it so much easier for you (see, I just love WordPress!).

You can simply install a plug-in that helps you turn your page into a sales page.

You can then simply copy and paste your copy as a regular page and place an order link of the product you're selling.

Once the customer clicks on it, he or she will be redirected to a payment processing page, where he or she can place an order and pay.

You can also choose among the paid plug-ins available. Now before you complain about spending more, you should know how powerful they are:

Sales page Plugins

http://easywpsalespages.com/ - This is perfect for people who lack visual abilities.

You don't have to think about how to format your sales page as this product carries multitudes of in-built designs you will be done with your sales page in minutes (true).

There is also a variety of cutesy and colorful Add to Cart buttons just to enhance the aesthetic appeal of your page.

http://www.flexsqueeze.com/category/squeeze-pages/ - There are fewer templates to choose here, but what it lacks in number it makes up with its design.

Theirs are truly professional looking.

What's more, they are categorized according to the type of call to action or message you want to send to your potential customers.

Moreover, the sales page can also function like a blog, so you're hitting two birds with one stone with this one.

Take note, though, that the price can be very hefty. It costs more than a hundred dollars.

http://www.wpsqueezepage.com/ - It produces very neat sales page, easy to install, quite cheap at $47, and doesn't give you any headache during customization.

However, this doesn't work in any of the templates of FlexSqueeze.

You can also check out other great choices:

http://creationspire.com/wpspire/ (for more advanced Internet marketers) and http://www.WordPressppc.com/

19. How To Take Payments On Your WordPress Website Sales page

Now the easiest way to collect money on your sales page is using good old PayPal.com or stripe.
Let's talk about PayPal first.

With this WordPress PayPal Plugin you do not need a shopping cart.

20. WordPress Simple PayPal Shopping Cart Plugin

Sell anything from your WordPress website easily.

The WordPress Simple PayPal Shopping Cart is a very easy to use and lightweight WordPress plugin that allows you to sell products or services online in one click from your WordPress blog.

Plugin Description

WordPress Simple PayPal Shopping Cart lets you add an 'Add to Cart' button anywhere on your blog.

This plugin also allows you to add the shopping cart anywhere in a post or page or sidebar easily.

The shopping cart shows the user what they currently have in the cart and allows them to add or remove items.

The payment is processed by PayPal.

Screenshots

Simple Product Display

My Cool Ebook
Price: $19.95

ADD TO CART

Product Display With Variation Control Product Display Box.

Below is a screenshot of the shopping cart when item is added to it.

Get the plugin here->https://wordpress.org/plugins/wordpress-simple-paypal-shopping-cart/

21. Okay now about Stripe Payment Processor

Here's a quick rundown of some features Stripe has set up for you to work with:
• Stripe Checkout: Saves you from having to design forms

and payment flows from scratch, but also allows for a high level of customization.

Unlike a basic PayPal account, your customers stay on your page the entire time, and unlike the PayPal Pro account (which gives you the hosted page), all PCI compliance is handled for you.

Checkout is a very big asset to merchants.

- Mobile commerce integration: Stripe provides documentation for
Android or iOS to power in-app payments. There's also a one-touch solution that enables users to save their data for faster
purchases next time.
- Subscription solutions: This includes unlimited options for plan types.
You can even subscribe a single user to multiple plan types. Upgrading subscribers to higher tiers is easy.

 This is another feature that actually works in favor of everyday
merchants, and it's provided at no charge for merchants (compared to $30-$40 for PayPal).

- Coupons and free trials: Stripe provides great marketing tools, made easy. Entice would-be customers to take the plunge by setting up a free trial period or providing a special offer.
- Advanced reporting: Download your choice of reports, or send data to QuickBooks or Xero.
- Bitcoin integration: Pay just 0.5% per transaction. • Stripe Connect: Connect is a suite of tools designed specifically for marketplaces.

Stripe supports more than 100 currencies and automatically converts them.

You can also use Connect to verify international sellers, add descriptor text that appears on credit card statements, and automate payments for marketplace sellers or create a custom payment schedule.

On top of that, you can now also automatically route payments as they come in by linking a charge a recipient. Stripe will handle the rest.

22. Stripe WordPress Plugin

Full Stripe (Free Edition) WordPress plugin is designed to make it easy for you to accept payments from your WordPress site.

Powered by Stripe, you can embed payment forms into any post or page and take payments directly from your website without making your customers leave for a 3rd party website.

The free edition of WP Full Stripe has the following features:

1. Create payment forms to take payments via Stripe.
2. Drop payment forms on any page or post with a simple short code that you just place anywhere on the page to insert other content.
3. Choose between set price and donation style payment forms.
4. View list of received payment details from within WordPress.
5. Choose to send email receipts on successful payment, via Stripe.
6. Choose to redirect to a page/post following successful payment.
7. Customize forms with extra custom fields, email address and billing address.
8. Ajax style forms with no page redirects to take payments.
9. Create multiple versions of payment forms to suit your needs.

Upgrading to the paid version of WP Full Stripe will give you these extra features:

1. Create recurring subscription plans from within WordPress.
2. Sign up users to recurring subscriptions.
3. Full customizable subscription forms to drop on any page or post.
4. View list of subscribers and plans from within WordPress.
5. Create bank transfers (US Only).
6. Use Stripe Checkout style popup & responsive forms.
7. Fully customize Stripe Checkout forms to include things like custom image and "remember-me" option.
8. Add custom fields to payment & subscription forms.
9. Improved UI and WordPress integration.
10. Easily add custom CSS on your forms.
11. Send custom email payment receipts with dynamic content.
12. Regular updates and feature additions.
13. Premium support.

23. Quick Tips

Here are some quick tips.

Because of the many options and the possibility of marketing with great ease, it's so easy for you to get caught up or feel overwhelmed by the numerous tools available.

It's more fun to play with the designs and themes, I know. However, it's the content that matters.

Do take time to learn how to write a good and compelling sales copy.

It's not possible for me to cover copywriting here, so if you want to learn just look around your competition or search Google for good converting sales pages.

Here are few tips for you to begin with:
· Know the audience. When you know who you are selling too, you can set the right tone.

· Add magic words. You can always get the attention of Internet users when you have "free," "secret," and "top product," among others, in the title or anywhere in your sales letter.

· Include testimonials. If you've gone through beta testing, add the reactions or feedback to further strengthen the claims you've made.

· Focus on the benefits. People are interested in products they need. So, you need to answer the question "What's in it for me?" in your sales page.

· Go for facts. Back up your claims with proven research, and don't say anything you cannot substantiate later.

24. Affiliate Marketing - No Product Needed!

If you do not have a product to sell this is for you.

Let's talk about the wonderful world of affiliate marketing.
When I decided to earn money using a WordPress blog/website, this was the field that I got into.

And so far, I have never regretted this. One of the things I love about affiliate marketing is I don't need to have any product of my own or keep any inventory.

I don't have to be mindful of any physical orders. However, I can still be a salesperson—and a good one at that.

For those who aren't familiar with affiliate marketing, let me provide you with some background.

An affiliate is someone who is connected to a much bigger entity.

For example, I could be an affiliate to Dresses.com, which sells gorgeous gowns.

Anyway, but that doesn't mean I am a full-time employee of the organization.

I earn through commissions and other methods of earning, including fixed rate or percentage of sales.

For me to start earning, though, I need to promote the products of the said company.

That's what affiliate marketing is all about.

To find affiliate products just google "product type + affiliate program", or for digital products go to clickbank.com (to learn how to make money selling clickbank digital products go here- https://keithjunor.com/clickbank) and to find physical products to sell go to cj.com (commission junction)

Now you are going to learn about ways to get traffic from the social networks like Facebook.com:

1. WordPress allows you to install social network plug-ins such as Facebook (http://WordPress.org/extend/plugins/wp-facebookconnect/) and Twitter (http://WordPress.org/extend/plugins/twitter-tools/).

This way, all those who are in my Facebook and Twitter Friends' list can receive instant updates and can also view and send comments about my entries.

Simply put, you spend less time on creating your affiliate site and more time promoting.

You can turn your WordPress into a review site selling other peoples products (clickbank, commission junction etc.)

What does this mean?
It's similar to affiliate marketing but this one is more dedicated and provides details about the product and it's competition.

Review sites convert very well because the visitor doesn't have to do much research, as it's already done by the reviewer (that's you!)

All you have to do is to deliver your expert opinion about it.

It's one of the best ways to earn money because writing reviews enhances your credibility.

Combine this with affiliate marketing, and you can expect your conversion rate to increase dramatically.
Review Site Tips

· You may want to use this plug-in:
http://WordPressreviewplugins.com.

It greatly improves your review by allowing you to create comparison tables, import information from any kind of database, develop star ratings, and can work with any WordPress theme.

· Gather as much information as you can. Your reviews should not be based solely on mere opinions. You need to provide your review with the facts.

If you can, interview experts, read journals, and watch videos provide your own screenshots, photos etc..
· Be honest.

There's no other way to be trusted than that. Honesty is important because your customers are not going to come back if you have misled them in any way.

If you recommend a product that doesn't really work, you're damaging your name and the product you're selling. Heck, you may even find yourself in a lawsuit.

25. Membership Sites

Let's learn a little about membership sites.

There are two important questions that need to be answered about membership websites:

Why should you opt for content management system?
Why should you use WordPress?
Why content management system?

The main motivation for Internet users to sign up to a membership website is they want to have access to exclusive information.

So far, the best way of presenting this information is through a content management system. With it, you can easily add new content, rearrange them, and combine various media files: texts, videos, and audio.

You can also easily manage the content.

You can add, modify, or delete content and you don't have to be a programmer or an HTML expert to do that.

You can also encourage interaction among members through feedback forms.

Why Use WordPress?

Based on my experience, WordPress offers great flexibility managing content and there are quite a few good plugins that can turn your WordPress CMS (Customer Management System) into a full-fledged membership site while protecting your members only content.

Protecting your content is the utmost priority if you are running membership websites.

The entire program is useless if the public gets to see the information.

These plugins permit you to protect premium posts with a lot of additional flexibility.

Just to give you an idea what they are, check out some examples below:

Wishlist Member (http://WordPressmembershipplugins.net/wishlist-member/) –

It is very easy to install, and offers the following: download protection, payment system, content delivery, partial content protection, autoresponder integration, protected RSS feeds, affiliate program, and available membership levels.

It also offers extensive customer support and 30-day money-back guarantee

Members Only (http://WordPress.org/extend/plugins/members-only/) – It helps control the posts that are meant to be exclusive. Posts remain hidden unless the Internet users signs up or logs in.

HidePost (http://WordPress.org/extend/plugins/hidepost/) – It hides certain aspects of the posts. Only the members can have full access to them.

User Access Manager

(http://www.gm-alex.de/projects/WordPress/plugins/user-acces s-manager/) –

It gives you a lot of freedom on how you want to manage user access and the membership website.

You may also visit http://www.ryanlee.com. This guy maintains a membership website through a blogging platform.

26. The Audience Capture Method

Ok, I want to talk a little about Lead Generation.

If you're an Internet marketer, you don't promote your product to just about anyone.

You have to determine your market and attract the right people into your business.

These are the potential customers to whom you're going to sell.

WordPress can also be a very effective tool for lead generation.

First, as you've learned a few pages earlier, there are so many themes that will allow you to build your squeeze or landing pages on the fly.

You can also come up with a variety of them with various subscription forms depending on the submission habits of your Internet users.

Most definitely, there are a bunch of themes you can use, some of them available here: http://www.squeezetheme.com

27. Traffic Generation

We are going to talk about Traffic Generation, the lifeblood of any business.

When you're in cyberspace, traffic takes a whole new meaning.

It's common for people to get irked when they're stuck in traffic, but it's something you look forward to when you're in the World Wide Web.

Traffic means people, but they are not just any Internet user. These are the ones who visit your weblog, read your posts, click on your affiliate links, and purchase your products.

They are the ones who will refer your weblog to their friends and family, create reviews about your business, and just basically become a walking-talking ad.

They are your network connection. Without them, your business will die—and I'm sure of it.

There are plenty of conventional methods of driving traffic into your blog:

FREE Traffic Sources:

· Article marketing- write articles and post them on sites that accept articles- They also include a link back to your site for more info on your subject.

Checkout Slideshare.com and turn your content into a slideshow presentation for the world to see.

. Personal Facebook Page.

Facebook Business Page-can be linked to your website using a plugin called
· LinkedIn-allows you to sync your content on your personal profile. They will also notify you if readers subscribe to get new posts and updates.

· Blog marketing- getting your content on other blog websites as a guest poster-just go to the contact us page on related websites and offer to create an article for them. It should include a linkback to your website or a related page post.

-Blog commenting- making comments on related blog posts and including a link back to your website is a great way to get related free traffic.

Comment Hack- In google copy and paste the following script into the address bar using your niche keyword as the key phrase-> "title="CommentLuv Enabled"" KEYPHRASE

This will find pages of other WordPress sites that have a comment section that you can use to write a related comment AND add a clickable link back to your website.

Do this 10 times a day and you will see a stream of traffic to your site within a week or so and it will keep increasing as long as you continue.

· Social networking-posting on platforms like Facebook, Instagram, Twitter, Redditt, FB Page and more using the Jetpack Plugin-Settings-Sharing tab

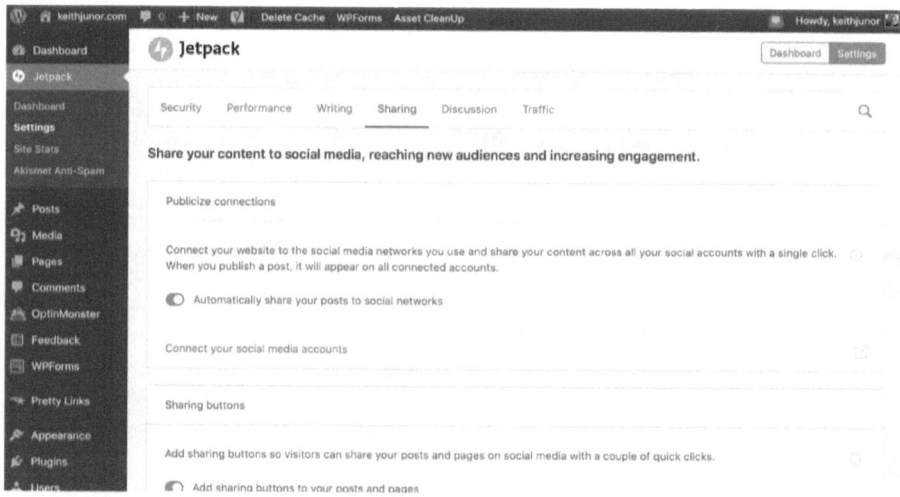

Then click "connect your social media accounts" and sign in to the social network sites you are signed up with.

Now when you create a post it will automatically send it to the social media sites you chose.

These are techniques that I use when I promote my websites. They do work, no doubt, but they also take so much of your time.

For instance, if you want to do article marketing, you have to write at least a 300-word article, which will take you around 30 minutes.
Then you have to submit the article to various article

directories and wait for around 24 to 48 hours before you will know if you get approved or not.

Paid Traffic:
- <u>Facebook Ads</u> (this is a subject that is too big to cover in this book so for training course on running Facebook ads for only $5 a day go to https://keithjunor.com/Facebook-ads
- Banner Ads-placing picture ads on the search engines and their affiliated networks. Only pay when someone clicks on the ad.
- Pay Per Click (also known as PPC ads) Ads on Google and BING/Yahoo (you place ads on the search networks and only pay when someone actually clicks on your ad.)

Great training on using PPC to sell affiliate products here https://keithjunor.com/ppc-affiliate-mktg

- Social Bookmarking using Onlywire.com (places your content on dozens of social sites automatically from your WordPress posts right after you publish them)

So, what I'm planning to show you is how you can drive traffic to your website with the least amount of time or money possible.

Remember, this is just a way to start and will never work as fast or as targeted as <u>paid advertising.</u>

You can do these through a number of plug-ins you can install into your WordPress site:

Tell-a-friend (http://WordPress.org/extend/plugins/search.php?q=tell+a+frien d) - Tell a Friend allows your Internet user to share the blog post or the weblog to their friends and family.

Another script you can use is http://plugins.trac.WordPress.org/wiki/wp-email. But what I like about Anup Raj's plug-in is you can customize it.

Digg Integrator (http://bill2me.com/digg-integrator/) – Digg has thousands of subscribers all over the world, and they are very active. When you become part of Digg, your content can be reviewed, shared, and rated by the rest of the members of the website.

With the integrator, Internet visitors who have Digg accounts can just click on the buttons, and your post can then be posted into their respective profiles.

The good news is that you can customize the appearance of the buttons, so they can add more appeal to your blog.

Chicklet Creator 2 (http://www.twistermc.com/social-bookmark-plugin/) – Okay, I do recommend that you integrate as many social networking websites as possible.

However, one of the biggest problems I faced was they overcrowded my weblog! It's a good thing I found this social plug-in.

Popular social networks are just in the drop-down menu, de-cluttering your pages.

Other Plug-ins:

· Google Analytics
http://WordPress.org/extend/plugins/google-analytics-for-wordpress/
· Subscription Options

http://WordPress.org/extend/plugins/subscription-options/
· Keywords Plug-in http://vapourtrails.ca/wp-keywords

· Social Traffic Monitor
http://WordPress.org/extend/plugins/social-traffic-monitor/

28. Last minute tips:

Make a Backup

Any time you make changes to your site it is a good idea to create a backup first. Making a backup is too easy to ignore and you can do it for free.

There are lots of free backup plugins available including UpdraftPlus Backup and Restoration, myRepono, WordPress Backup Plugin, BackWPup Free – WordPress Backup Plugin, Simple Backup, and many more.

There is even a backup option upgrade in Jetpack plugin.

Learn Facebook Marketing: right now this is the best way to get targeted traffic for any product or service, locally or worldwide but you can blow a lot of money trying to figure it out yourself.

Find good training at https://keithjunor.com/Facebook-ads

YouTube.com: create simple videos about your business/product/service and get them on YouTube for free advertising.

Get videos created at fiverr.com.

Learn about keywords, and YouTube search engine optimization and you could end up with thousands of views and visitors every month.

Get some YouTube training here

29. Conclusion

The most important thing you can do is TRY.

30. What's Next?

Just Do These Things:
You have now learned how to:

- choose a domain and webhost
- Connect them together
- Installing WordPress to your domain and hosting

- Tweaking it
- Adding media and content
- Creating a home page and menu bar
- Adding a contact form
- Changing themes
- The Plugin Functionality Formula.
- Setting up a sales page to sell any product or service

- How to take payments on your website
- Affiliate marketing with your site
- The Audience Capture Method
- Lead and traffic generation ideas
- Creating a review or Membership site

31. Your Goal

Now your goal is to get your website online and use themes and plugins to make it look and do what you want it to.

Since the initial installation of WordPress only takes a few minutes you should have the basic site up and running in less than 1 hour.

All that is left, other than adding your content, is to find the right theme then searching and installing the plugins to give you the functionality you need.

Since thousands of themes and plugins are available you will probably come up with other functions you need later on but please get the site online NOW and make changes as you go.

I know a lot of us have the tendency to want to keep making changes until we think it is perfect but the only one that matters is the customer and if your site is not live they cannot find you.

So, there is no reason that your website should not be up and running from day one.

I know people of all age groups, with virtually no technical skills that have followed these instructions and created multiple websites and made money promoting their products or services or an affiliate product.

You can also contact me if you decide not to build your own WordPress Website and I can build it for you from $199 and up depending on the complexity you desire.

Just click here and send me an email to keith@keithjunor.com or kbjunor@gmail.com

Visit my website at https://keithjunor.com/ for other ways to make money online.

I have also just released my newest book about setting and achieving goals on Amazon.

It is called "The Quantum Goals Achievement System" and it compiles 10 "Mind Hacks" for success in goal setting and achievement that I have learned from some of the top self-improvement guru's over the last 30 years of my career.

Please check out info about it here:
https://keithjunor.com/goals

Keith Junor

www.ingramcontent.com/pod-product-compliance
Lightning Source LLC
Chambersburg PA
CBHW020709180526
45163CB00008B/3006